NEW INITIATIVES IN CHRISTIAN INITIATION

Simon Vibert

Fellowship of Word and Spirit

ORTHOS

is a series of booklets from

Fellowship of Word and Spirit

Biblical Theology for the 21st Century
Series Editor: Lance Bidewell

Further copies of Orthos and information about the Fellowship may be obtained from:
Fellowship of Word and Spirit, The Vicarage, Warwick Bridge, Carlisle, Cumbria, England, CA4 8RF
http://www.st-james.org.uk/fws/

Printed in Great Britain by
Print-Out, Histon, Cambridge CB4 9JE

ISBN 1 874694 06 0

PREFACE

This Orthos is written with Fellowship of Word and Spirit's commitment to applied biblical theology in mind. What is the biblical theology of Holy Communion and how does this understanding of Communion apply to one current area of church life, namely the admission of children to Holy Communion?

There is a common perception that the issue of 'children receiving Communion prior to confirmation' is purely a matter to be discussed by Anglo-Catholics, who may hold a view of the sacraments which is different from evangelicals. If the efficacy of the bread and wine operate without conscious faith, then surely children may receive – indeed must receive – if they are to be built up in the faith.

Donald Allister's Reform booklet is rightly concerned about the pressure exerted within many dioceses to introduce a view of Holy Communion which would support this erroneous understanding of the sacraments.[1]

However, there are many within the Reformed tradition who advocate the reception of children to Communion prior to confirmation, and it is from a biblical-theological point of view that they reach their conclusions. This is a live debate, and a lively debate too, as our church discovered when we held our first public discussion of the subject. Many dioceses are encouraging churches to debate this matter at PCC level and are calling for a response.

How then do Reformed-minded evangelicals approach the subject? What issues are raised for those of us who hold to a Reformed view of the sacraments and a covenantal approach to Christian initiation?

In order to begin answering these questions I will spend some time thinking about the place of the sacraments in biblical theology. Next I try to summarize the position in which modern Anglicans find themselves by looking at the recent General Synod Reports on Christian initiation and responding to them.[2] Finally I aim to synthesize these two sections into a coherent approach to the subject.

A BIBLICAL THEOLOGY OF HOLY COMMUNION

Transcript of a sermon preached at St Luke's, Wimbledon Park

Luke 22:1-22

1   Now the Feast of Unleavened Bread, called the Passover, was approaching,
2   and the chief priests and the teachers of the law were looking for some way to get rid of Jesus, for they were afraid of the people.
3   Then Satan entered Judas, called Iscariot, one of the Twelve.
4   And Judas went to the chief priests and the officers of the temple guard and discussed with them how he might betray Jesus.
5   They were delighted and agreed to give him money.
6   He consented, and watched for an opportunity to hand Jesus over to them when no crowd was present.
7   Then came the day of Unleavened Bread on which the Passover lamb had to be sacrificed.
8   Jesus sent Peter and John, saying, 'Go and make preparations for us to eat the Passover.'
9   'Where do you want us to prepare for it?' they asked.
10 He replied, 'As you enter the city, a man carrying a jar of water will meet you. Follow him to the house that he enters,
11 and say to the owner of the house, "The Teacher asks: Where is the guest room, where I may eat the Passover with my disciples?"
12 He will show you a large upper room, all furnished. Make preparations there.'
13 They left and found things just as Jesus had told them. So they prepared the Passover.
14 When the hour came, Jesus and his apostles reclined at the table.
15 And he said to them, 'I have eagerly desired to eat this Passover with you before I suffer.
16 For I tell you, I will not eat it again until it finds fulfilment in the kingdom of God.'
17 After taking the cup, he gave thanks and said, 'Take this and divide it among you.
18 For I tell you I will not drink again of the fruit of the vine until the kingdom of God comes.'
19 And he took bread, gave thanks and broke it, and gave it to them, saying, 'This is my body given for you; do this in remembrance of me.'

20 In the same way, after the supper he took the cup, saying, 'This cup is the new covenant in my blood, which is poured out for you.
21 But the hand of him who is going to betray me is with mine on the table.
22 The Son of Man will go as it has been decreed, but woe to that man who betrays him.' (NIV)

1. Introduction

I am quite struck by the fact that the two visual aids which we recognize in the Protestant Church (more commonly known as sacraments) are actually both quite earthy and everyday pictures.

One picture is of something that most of us do on most days – washing – and probably more than once a day, unless you're a 7-year-old boy, when it is much less! This is the picture of baptism.

The other picture is of eating and drinking, which is something you do several times a day, unless you're a teenager, in which case you do it several times an hour, whilst many adults spend their time trying to eat less. However, I recently learnt some encouraging news for those of you who are trying to lose weight.

* If no one sees you eat it, then it has no calories, so that's OK.
* If you drink diet coke and eat chocolate, then they cancel each other out.
* When eating with someone else, calories don't count so long as the other person eats the same or more than you.
* Food used for medicinal purposes never counts. Such medicinal food includes brandy, chocolate, cheesecake.
* If you fatten up everyone else around you, you of course look thinner.
* Food you eat (such as popcorn) whilst watching a film doesn't count because it's merely part of the entertainment.

More seriously, taking this very earthy illustration of eating was natural for Jesus. There is nothing particularly mystical about it, although of course we need to understand the Passover context surrounding Luke 22. But even then, the killing of a lamb and eating it, whilst later very pregnant with meaning, at the time was a fairly normal culinary pastime.

With this in mind I want to ask the question 'What happens at Holy Communion?'. There are a number of words we use within Anglicanism to describe it. The words 'Holy Communion' have the idea of fellowship or *koinonia*, associated with the fellowship meal or love feast celebrated in the New Testament. There is the more formal word 'eucharist', which is not a word I like very much because it has other connotations, but really it just means 'a thanksgiving' or 'a celebration'. I think the best words are 'The Lord's Supper'. They are more biblical and are the ones used by the *Book of Common Prayer* which introduces the service as 'Holy Communion otherwise known as "The Lord's Supper"'.

The background to the Lord's Supper is very important and I want to spend a few moments looking at Exodus 12, the first celebration of the Passover meal. The context in which the meal was eaten is very important, since it was in preparation for the last of act of judgement upon Pharaoh and the people of Egypt for not letting Moses and the people go to worship God. Through the act of judgement, God liberates his people. The last judgement is far worse than blood, frogs, flies, plagues, boils, hail, locusts or darkness. It is the judgement on the firstborn, the heir of the family.

God will come down in judgement, but this will also mean salvation for God's elect. Let us look at a few things in the text of Exodus 12 :

1   The LORD said to Moses and Aaron in Egypt

2   'This month is to be for you the first month, the first month of your year.

3   Tell the whole community of Israel that on the tenth day of this month each man is to take a lamb for his family, one for each household.

4   If any household is too small for a whole lamb, they must share one with their nearest neighbour, having taken into account the number of people there are. You are to determine the amount of lamb needed in accordance with what each person will eat.

5   The animals you choose must be year-old males without defect, and you may take them from the sheep or the goats.

6   Take care of them until the fourteenth day of the month, when all the people of the community of Israel must slaughter them at twilight.

7   Then they are to take some of the blood and put it on the sides and tops of the door-frames of the houses where they eat the lambs.

8   That same night they are to eat the meat roasted over the fire, along with bitter herbs, and bread made without yeast.

9   Do not eat the meat raw or cooked in water, but roast it over the fire – head, legs and inner parts.

10   Do not leave any of it till morning; if some is left till morning, you must burn it.

11   This is how you are to eat it: with your cloak tucked into your belt, your sandals on your feet and your staff in your hand. Eat it in haste; it is the LORD's Passover.

12   On that same night I will pass through Egypt and strike down every firstborn –

both men and animals – and I will bring judgement on all the gods of Egypt. I am the LORD.

13   The blood will be a sign for you on the houses where you are; and when I see the blood, I will pass over you. No destructive plague will touch you when I strike Egypt.

14   This is a day you are to commemorate; for the generations to come you shall celebrate it as a festival to the LORD – a lasting ordinance.

15   For seven days you are to eat bread made without yeast. On the first day remove the yeast from your houses, for whoever eats anything with yeast in it from the first day until the seventh must be cut off from Israel.

16   On the first day hold a sacred assembly, and another one on the seventh day. Do no work at all on these days, except to prepare food for everyone to eat – that is all you may do.' (NIV)

2. Passover

Notice God's explanation of the significance of the Passover:

2.1 First, there is the process of selecting and finding the lamb, then killing it and pasting the blood of the lamb on the doorposts. By doing this, God's chosen people are identified and set apart from everybody else.

2.2 Secondly, the lamb that died would act as a substitute for the firstborn child in the Israelite household, and when God saw the blood, he would 'pass over' the house, which is all the word 'Passover' means.

2.3 Thirdly, notice verse 30, which says 'Pharaoh and all his officials and all the Egyptians got up during the night, and there was loud wailing in Egypt, for there was not a house without someone dead.' This was true for the people of Israel – there wasn't a house without someone dead, because in the houses of the Israelites there was a dead lamb instead of the firstborn. By offering the blood of the lamb in their place, the firstborn was spared.

What a wonderful picture of the atonement. Sin was punished. Death still happened, but in their household a substitute took the place of the firstborn child. The result of this was not only that they were passed over in judgement, but they were actually released from slavery. As they celebrated the Passover in those gruesome circumstances, they thereby escaped from the tyranny of Egypt and were redeemed from slavery.

2.4 Fourthly, this event was so significant for Israel, that it became a permanent memorial of sacrifice, of praise and thanksgiving.

2.5 I would like you to notice how the Passover theme is developed in the New Testament. Christ, the Lamb of God, is selected (1 Peter 2:4), tested (Luke 4; Heb. 4:15), sacrificed as a substitute (1 Cor. 5:5), and we benefit by our participation (1 Cor. 10:16f.).

At the cross, two things happened. The Lamb of God was judged by God, dying in our place and taking the judgement we deserve. He is 'the Lamb of God who takes away the sin of the world' (John 1:29). But, continuing the parallel, the cross was also the new Exodus, the very means of salvation. God found a way to execute justice perfectly in judging sin, by judging his son in our place. Yet at the time he could be merciful towards us and offer us salvation. This is an amazing picture, demonstrating how God would judge his sinless Son and thereby save sinful people. God is both 'just and justifier' (Rom. 3:21ff.)

The celebration of Passover in Jewish history looked back to God's great redemption. Every time they celebrated it, they would recall that momentous liberating event. But there was also a looking forward as well to a day when there would be a lamb that would take away sins for ever, hence John's exclamation 'Behold the Lamb of God!'. At last 'a Lamb of God who takes away the sin of the world' - God's Passover lamb (1 Cor. 5:7). He would not now spare us from judgement in Egypt but actually spare us from the wrath of God ultimately.

Just as the Passover looked back to an historic, momentous, once-for-all act of salvation, so similarly the same picture language is used to describe the Lord's Supper. This looks backwards to the once-for-all momentous event of salvation. In fact, both of the sacraments – baptism and the Lord's Supper – point backwards to the cross. They are visual aids of what Jesus did there in our place.

One passing thought struck me as being interesting here. Notice in Exodus 12 the balance between denial and celebration, feasting and fasting. They would eat unleavened bread; they would eat it in haste, but yet they were also to consume and enjoy this lamb. It was a balance maintained through their history, involving periods of sacrifice, abstention from food or eating unleavened bread, but ending the time with festivals of great celebration. Actually that should be a balance in the Christian life as well. We go through periods of denial and disciplining ourselves – of pummelling our bodies, as Paul puts it – in order to bring ourselves into line, and that is appropriate and right. But that is not the end of it because there should be the feasting at the end of the fasting, culminating in celebration and joy as well. The balanced Christian life is a combination of those two, which I think is given us in picture form in the Lord's Supper.   We do not partake to fill our stomachs (1 Cor. 11:33ff. warns against this) but we anticipate a great future banquet in heaven (1 Cor. 11:26; Rev. 19).

3. Holy Communion

What was Christ doing when he celebrated the Passover with his disciples? Clearly, Jesus interpreted and applied the Passover meal as he instituted the Lord's Supper. What does this do to our understanding of Holy Communion? Let us focus on Luke 22, but also allow this passage to give us a theological application of the role of Holy Communion for today.

The events leading up to Jesus' crucifixion match uncannily with the preparation for the Passover. I agree with many commentators who suggest that the disciples celebrated the Passover the day before everybody else in Jerusalem. The Passover proper was in fact being prepared as Jesus died on the cross. Notice, for example, that they only had bread and wine: they did not have the lamb present there for their meal.[3]

The following day, the Passover lambs were to be slaughtered. In accordance with Exodus 12 the high priest performed dozens of checks on the animal to ensure that it was perfect, before being slaughtered. It was at this point that Jesus was examined by Pilate, who concluded, 'I find no basis for charge against him' (John 19:6).

According to this chronology, Jesus died on the cross as the lambs were being slain in the temple. John 19:36 observes, 'These things happened so that the Scripture would be fulfilled, "not one of his bones will be broken"'. That quote from Exodus 12:46 refers to the treatment of the Passover lamb that not one of his bones will be broken. Isn't it striking that John applies these words to Jesus' death? Anxious because Passover is approaching, they plan to break the victims' legs but find that Jesus is already dead, and then John quotes Exodus 12:46.

Paul tells us: 'Christ our Passover lamb has been sacrificed' (1 Cor. 5:7). Similarly in Hebrews 9:28 we read: 'Christ was sacrificed once to take away the sins of many people'.

With this historical context in mind, let us pause to consider what the New Testament writers tell us about Jesus' intention in instituting the Lord's Supper. For it becomes clear that it was never intended that the meal which Jesus celebrated with his disciples recorded in Luke 22, would be a perpetual sacrifice.

3.1 One sacrifice

Christ gave us this renewed meal because it reminds us that there is only one sacrifice. The one sacrifice for sins was made by the lamb of God who takes away the sin of the world. Indeed, he who in just a few hours would offer himself on the altar of the cross, gave a visual anticipation of it in the meal the night before.

When Jesus said 'This is my body given for you...This cup is the new covenant in my blood, which is poured out for you' (Luke 22:19f.), his attention was not upon the bread they ate and the wine they drank, but upon the cross which cast its shadow over their proceedings. Consequently I understand Jesus as not referring to future perpetual acts of sacrifice going on down the history of the church. Rather, he was talking about one sacrifice, the sacrifice he is about to make on the cross.

3.1.1 One practical consequence of this is that it is important that we use appropriate language when we gather to break bread and drink wine. First, I don't think we should use the word 'priest', for that is an inappropriate word for my job. Admittedly the *Book of Common Prayer* does use 'priest', but it also explains that the priest is a presbyter – the link with the Latin root of the word. In other words, the *BCP* assumed this to be an elder, a teaching pastor.

3.1.2 Secondly, I don't think that we should use the word 'altar' (this word is not used in the *BCP*), because the table at the top of the church building is not a place where a sacrifice is being made: rather it is a place where a meal is being prepared. One of the reasons why we bring the table down and among the congregation is because we want to emphasize that we share a communal meal. There is no sacrifice happening. The whole point of the sacrament is that it is to be visible and among the people.

3.1.3 Thirdly, recognize the appropriate place of the sacrificial language at Communion. When we say those words 'Yours Lord is the greatness, the power, the glory, the splendour and the majesty', I only hold up the money as an offering. I'm not offering bread and wine to God as some sort of sacrifice to him: I am just laying the table for a meal together. The only prayer of sacrifice is made at the end of the service when we offer our souls and bodies as living sacrifices (see Romans 12:1f.).

3.1.4 Fourthly, consider the layout of the church for this meal. Many Anglican churches are designed according to a pattern that is more in line with an Old Testament temple than it is with a New Testament church. The 'high altar' language mirrors the Holy of Holies in the temple. When we did have a chance to play around a little with the architecture at my last church, we created a half circle so that we could face one another rather than just face forward. Little things speak volumes about what we understand is going on. We wanted to communicate that the central point of the Lord's Supper was eating and drinking in the presence of the fellowship of believers.

There is only one sacrifice, and the meal that God has given us to eat is an active visual aid to help us to appreciate this. I am not trying to make light of Communion, because it *is* a wonderful celebration meal if you understand it in that context. But its purpose is to help us appreciate and apply that one sacrifice made for us.

3.1.5. *Is Christ really present in the Lord's Supper?*

The official doctrine of the Church of England is that Christ is 'really present' in the

Lord's Supper, living in the hearts of believers who eat and drink by faith, not in the bread, but in Christ. Arguably the greatest Anglican theologian was Richard Hooker. He said: 'The real presence of Christ's most blessed body and blood is not to be sought for in the sacrament but in the worthy receiver of the sacrament'.

Coming to Holy Communion will do you no good if your heart is not right with God. That is why I use the phrase of invitation: 'You are welcome to the Lord's table if you know and love the Lord and if you are living in peace and harmony with your neighbour'. If you do not know and love the Lord and if you are not living in peace and harmony with your neighbour, 1 Corinthians 11 warns that coming to the Lord's Supper will result in judgement from God, partly because you are assuming that the sacraments work apart from the need for reconciled relationships between God and man, and among men.

But, when we receive bread and wine with our hearts right before the Lord and with our minds conscious both of one another and with a remembrance of what he did on our behalf in the past and with an anticipation of the day when we will all eat it together in heaven, *then* Christ is really present amongst his people, because they are enlivened by the act of eating and drinking and thereby feeding spiritually upon Jesus and all his benefits! So we should come with great expectations at Communion, because if our hearts are prepared and we eat 'acknowledging the body' (the body of Christ, that is the physical body of gathered people), then this is a wonderful corporate experience that we should celebrate together.

3.2 One memorial

There is one memorial, an act of remembrance. When Jesus said 'do this in remembrance of me' (Luke 22:19), he is calling them and us to remember, not now the old Passover, but the new Passover, Calvary. Passover was so named because God passed over every house that had the lamb's blood smeared on the doorframe. The blood indicated that judgement in that house had already taken place, for the lamb had died as a substitute. God judged the lamb in place of the firstborn. Similarly God passed over judging us, and instead shed the blood of his Son, our substitute.

If you were asked the question 'When are we saved?', how would you go about answering that? Are we saved at the moment we believed? Are we saved on the last day? Or were we saved the moment Christ died? Well I guess the answer to all three of those questions is 'yes'. We were saved at the moment when Jesus Christ paid the ransom price for our sins. We were saved at the point when we came to appropriate that for ourselves, when God arrested us and called us to repent of our sins and to trust in Jesus.

But ultimately we are not saved until judgement day, when God will call every person to account before him. On that day we will plead the blood of Jesus given on our behalf, and the moment in history when we came to trust that for ourselves. The New Testament talks in terms of the verdict of judgement day being read back into the present. More on this in a moment.

Salvation is based upon these three realities, and there is a sense in which the Lord's Supper involves that three-way focus. It involves *looking back* to what Christ has done once for all on my behalf. It involves *looking around* to the community of believers amongst whom we share this meal. And it involves *looking forward* to the day when we will drink anew in the kingdom.

Jesus said, 'I have eagerly desired to eat this Passover with you before I suffer. For I tell you, I will not eat it again until it finds fulfilment in the kingdom of God' (vv.15b-16). I have always interpreted this to mean: 'I won't eat this again until I get to heaven and be with my Father', which at one level is right. But it is interesting to notice that the final great celebratory meal, the wedding supper of the lamb recorded in Revelation 19, only happens when Christ gathers in all the elect from all nations. His mission purpose is finally accomplished, and people from every language, tongue and tribe will worship him.

I think that it is this event which Jesus is anticipating in Luke 22. In effect he says: 'That's when we'll celebrate; we'll have a great party in heaven because that's when I'll eat again, when the work is finally accomplished'. What he is signifying that night at the meal table and accomplishing the following day on the cross, will one day be fulfilled in the kingdom. Then he adds this: 'I'm not going to eat it until that day comes. You eat it to remember me and keep your hope strong and empower yourselves for mission, but I'm going to wait until I can eat it anew with you and with all the ransomed that I will gather from every tongue and tribe and people and nation'.

This sense of impetus and missionary zeal should be borne in mind as we prepare for Communion. First, we confess our sin and renew our faith in God's justifying death for ourselves. But then, secondly, we ask God to give us the heart of Christ for the coming of his kingdom and for the completion of his cause. In this way we are caught up in an expectation that one day we will eat it with a multitude of people from every language, tongue, tribe and nation who have been brought into the kingdom of God.

We look back in gratitude and say 'thank you' that the victory has already been won by Christ. We look forward in anticipation that he will provide battle rations for the mopping-up operation until the great day of feasting and celebration at the end of the age.

3.3 Two sacraments

Both baptism and the Lord's Supper enliven our understanding of what Christ did for us in His death on the cross, and how we may be partakers spiritually of that event. We sometimes use the phrase 'the sacraments being outward signs of inward realities'.

John Calvin described the sacraments as being 'The Visible Words'. Cranmer reflected this in the rubric in the *Book of Common Prayer* and the 39 Articles. The liturgy is so shaped to emphasize the importance of feeding on Christ by faith and it assumes that a sermon is preached, or the homilies read, in order that word and sacrament be married together. The visible words are to be accompanied by the spoken words, and the visible and verbal give eloquent testimony to each other.

Jesus said: 'Do this in remembrance of ... not your past deliverance from Egypt ... do it in remembrance of me'. They are audacious words – if you think about it. Imagine that you were with the disciples celebrating that Passover with Jesus. He calls attention to his body, not the lamb's body. And whilst he makes a close connection between the bread and wine and his body and blood, they would not have taken the bread and said 'we are going to be eating your flesh literally, and drinking your blood literally'.

The Protestant Church only recognizes two sacraments – namely baptism and the Lord's Supper. They are a 'means of grace' insofar as they point us to a gracious God who achieved so much for us on the cross and offers strength and equipment until the work is done.

3.4   Summary and implications from 1 Corinthians 11 : 23 - 34

23   For I received from the Lord what I also passed on to you: The Lord Jesus, on the night he was betrayed, took bread,

24   and when he had given thanks, he broke it and said, 'This is my body, which is for you; do this in remembrance of me.'

25   In the same way, after supper he took the cup, saying, 'This cup is the new covenant in my blood; do this, whenever you drink it, in remembrance of me'.

26   For whenever you eat this bread and drink this cup, you proclaim the Lord's death until he comes.

27   Therefore, whoever eats the bread or drinks the cup of the Lord in an unworthy manner will be guilty of sinning against the body and blood of the Lord.

28 A man ought to examine himself before he eats of the bread and drinks of the cup.

29 For anyone who eats and drinks without recognising the body of the Lord eats and drinks judgement on himself.

30 That is why many among you are weak and sick, and a number of you have fallen asleep.

31 But if we judged ourselves, we would not come under judgement.

32 When we are judged by the Lord, we are being disciplined so that we will not be condemned with the world.

33 So then, my brothers, when you come together to eat, wait for each other.

34 If anyone is hungry, he should eat at home, so that when you meet together it may not result in judgement. And when I come I will give further directions.

3.4.1 Look back (vv.23-24)

On the night before Jesus' death they were at the Passover meal, celebrating God's great past deliverance. We too look back: not to Egypt and the death of the lamb, but rather to Christ, our Passover lamb, who was sacrificed for us (1 Cor 5:7).

3.4.2 Look up (vv.19-22)

This is a simple meal at which the host is not visibly present – but really present in the hearts of believing people. The risen Christ is the head of the table and we come to feed *on* and *with* him. We come as his guests, looking to God to nourish our souls spiritually.

Notice that three times Paul uses the word 'bread'. He does not say that we eat the body of Jesus. He says that we eat bread. There is no change in the substance of the bread or the wine. The bread remains bread; the wine remains wine. Article 28 states that the sacraments do not operate apart from faith.[4]

3.4.3 Look in (vv.27-28)

This passage records a serious call to self-examination. Paul in 1 Corinthians 5 talked about the hunt for leaven – a family joke in Jewish households, with a serious message of the need for genuine repentance. Leaven symbolized the swelling of pride: that is why we hear the commandments right at the beginning of this service.

It is possible that you may eat to your damnation (v.27) if you are not repentant. If the sacraments operated apart from faith, that would not be possible. There is something going on in the heart of the believer which makes the sacrament effectual.

Let me illustrate. People sometimes draw the analogy between taking medicine and receiving Holy Communion. I am sin-sick and I come to take God's prescription for my spiritual health. However, I think the analogy is imperfect. When I take medicine, whether I believe it works or not (leaving aside psychosomatic or placebo effect for now!), it does the job. If I have a headache and I take paracetomol, it generally brings relief, it irrespective of whether I believe it works or not.

However, the Lord's Supper is not like that. If I eat unworthily, then it actually does me harm. The covenant language of the Lord's Supper includes promises for obedience and threats of judgement for the unrepentant. Consequently I must examine myself before I eat the bread and drink of the cup. The preparation in the *Book of Common Prayer* takes the warnings in 1 Corinthians very seriously and charges the would-be communicant to prepare carefully.

3.4.4 Look around (v.29)

'Recognizing' or 'discerning' the body, refers not to the physical body of Jesus but rather to the body of the church, as the following context (12:12ff.) makes clear.

Part of the repentance we have just referred to implies that if you are out of harmony with your brother/sister, then it is not enough just to abstain from communion. You are to go and make peace with them before you come to the table.

This text also implies that when we come to our discussion on the admission of children to Communion, they must at least have some ability to exercise that discernment.

3.4.5 Look forward (v.26)

This is our foretaste of heaven: we look forward to the day when there will be more than tokens. There will be a banquet at the marriage feast of the Lamb (Rev. 19). 'Maranatha' – come Lord Jesus – we want the reality!

3.4.6 Look outward (v.26)

Every Communion is an opportunity to tell the gospel in a compact summary form! To this extent the Lord's Supper issues gospel warnings and promises in the language of covenantal invitation!

Parameters for further discussion

The understanding of Holy Communion which we have outlined raises a number of issues which lead into our discussion about the admission of children to Communion. Two main questions which need to be answered include:

1. Who is eligible to receive the Lord's Supper?

We have assumed that baptism and the Lord's Supper are covenantal signs of belonging. Consequently the assumption is made that these signs belong to believers and their children. However this raises a number of subsequent questions:

a) How do we decide who 'belongs' to the covenant community of the church?

b) Should Holy Communion be given to all those who are members of the covenant community?

c) How may we take seriously the charge to prepare oneself through repentance and self-examination? And at what age do we deduce that covenant children are able 'discern the body'?

At what age can children look back, up, in, around, forward and outward?

2. How may we best prepare for Holy Communion in the life of the church?

This second question relates to the nurture of children and adults. It asks questions about how a biblical understanding of Holy Communion is to be reached, and how preparation should be made for each service and celebration of the Lord's Supper. Again we notice a number of changes in the life of the church.

How different the modern scene is from that of the seventeenth and eighteenth centuries. Charles Simeon was converted while studying at Kings College, Cambridge in 1779. He was warned about receiving Communion in the college chapel on Easter Day, and this so terrified him that he read a weighty book on our moral obligations entitled *The Whole Duty of Man* , which made him even more miserable! Then it came to him that he could transfer his guilt to another, and so he received assurance and that Easter had a special and new meaning for him. He became the vicar of Holy Trinity Church at the age of 22 and stayed there for 50 years. This remarkable ministry began partly as a consequence of the serious way in which the call to receive Holy Communion was made!

It is not just the theology of the *BCP* which runs contrary to modern culture. The assumptions made by the *BCP*, and the seriousness with which eighteenth-century English people approached Holy Communion, are not part of our church or wider culture. As we turn to consider the biblical requirements for preparation and nurture of young people in the life of the church, we need to recognize changes in our culture and ecclesiastical outlook, but at the same time to wrestle with some of the biblical principles of preparation and nurture which we have been considering in this section.

NEW INITIATIVES IN CHRISTIAN INITIATION

Discussions concerning the admission of children to Communion prior to confirmation within the Church of England have had a long history. Whilst the rubric of the 1662 *Book of Common Prayer* Communion service prohibits any but confirmed adults receiving Communion, it has been common to invite believers of all traditions to receive, and in the last three decades there has been increasing pressure to allow any baptised but unconfirmed congregation members to come to the Lord's Table.

Before we return to some of the questions raised at the end of section one, I propose to examine the history of the debate as it is discussed in the three main General Synod documents on the subject: *Communion before Confirmation* (1985), *Children in the Way* (1988), and *On the Way* (1995). This will give us a clearer picture of the current thinking about the subject in the Church of England today.

1. *Communion before Confirmation (CBC)*

CBC, published by the working party of the General Synod, was commissioned to discuss the 1976 Resolution of General Synod requesting a theological, sociological, historical and liturgical review of the place of Communion and confirmation in the life of the church. But even prior to this resolution, the 1969 'Ely' Commission concluded that baptism was a complete sacrament of Christian initiation and should provide a sufficient basis for admitting children to Communion prior to confirmation. The Commission published the report in 1971 entitled *Christian Initiation: Birth and Growth in the Christian Society* (see *CBC* pp. 1f.).

With the 'Ely' Commission's proposals established as a starting point, *CBC* went on to conclude that the Church of England should recognize that it is not absolutely necessary to be confirmed prior to being admitted to Communion. Confirmation should remain as a 'sacramental means of grace' but baptized persons may be admitted to communion prior to confirmation (p.49).

Practical suggestions were made for parishes to assist in the implementation of this policy, to which we shall return later (p.52). First we need to discuss the basis upon which this doctrinal statement about baptism and communion was made, namely that paedobaptism is a complete entry rite to full membership of the church.

We have already mentioned briefly the impact of the covenantal view that admission into the New Covenant is through baptism, which replaces the Old Covenant initiation rite of circumcision. Acts 2:41f. implies that baptized members are eligible to receive Communion, and 1 Corinthians 10 assumes that the baptized members of the congregation are sharing at the table.

However, neither of these two texts help convince the reader that junior members may be included in receiving bread and wine. Indeed, rather like the argument for paedobaptism itself, the argument is based upon covenant theological principles rather than isolated proof-texting.

The *CBC* report cites New Testament texts which imply the inclusion of children within God's kingdom (e.g. Mark 10:13-15; Acts 2:38f.; 10:47f.; 16:31; 1 Cor. 1) and from there gives historic evidence of the practice of baptizing children and assuming their inclusion at the Lord's Table. They summarize: 'To be capable of receiving baptism is to be capable of receiving Communion', although the references to John 3:5 (*unless one is born of water and the Spirit, he cannot enter the kingdom of God*) and John 6:53 (*unless you eat the flesh of the Son of Man and drink his blood, you have no life in you*) confuse the discussion, for they speak of initiation into the Christian community, and neither text is likely to have anything to do with the sacraments.

We are on safer ground in the consideration of covenantal initiation (circumcision being the outward sign of the Old Covenant and baptism being the outward sign of the New Covenant). The Commission is right to point out that these signs, being communal in nature, seem to imply that God deals with whole households rather than isolated individuals (see *CBC*, p.8f.).

However, the report fails to explore fully the implications of a covenantal understanding of baptism. The section on baptism and the reception of the Spirit (p.11f.) rightly recognizes that reception of the Spirit (or Baptism in/by the Holy Spirit) is tied to water baptism in the case of adults professing faith. The outward sign overflows from the inward experience. They are two sides of the same coin, although it would be clearer to say that water baptism follows inexorably on from baptism in the Spirit (i.e. conversion).

This is not inherently the case with the water baptism of children. The membership of God's covenant community is applied to children on the basis of the faith of the parents, but of course this requires subsequent ratification.

For this reason confirmation in the *Book of Common Prayer* was 'not now initiatory, not even a "booster" but a rite about continuing in grace' (p.16). The key objection given by the Council of Trent to allowing children to continue to receive Communion was that, though regeneration had taken place through the sacrament of baptism, children lacked the use of reason to receive the Communion. It is most likely for the same reason that Cranmer included the provision in the rubric of the *BCP* that 'there shall none be admitted to the Holy Communion, until such time as he can say the Catechism, and be Confirmed'. Confirmation became 'the certificate of instruction'.

The report calls into question whether the *BCP* rubric is sufficiently clear in a day and age where children are better educated, more integrated into the community, and have developed socially and psychologically. The argument is convincingly made that their understanding is at a more 'direct, affective' level, and excluding them from the Lord's Table when they may have a fairly thorough, albeit simplistic, devotion to Jesus may have damaging effects on their feeling of belonging and involvement in the Christian community.

Much of the impetus for a changed perspective on children and Communion has come as a result of their presence in the Sunday morning Communion service. They are no longer 'out of sight and out of mind' (which should never be appropriate surely?): rather they are often present in the Communion service itself. Since this report came out, the advent of more inclusive liturgies, particularly several of the alternative eucharistic prayers in *Common Worship,* seek to engage and involve the whole congregation in participation of the communal event. Along with the moves to admit children to Communion prior to confirmation, the issue has ceased to be 'At what age may children be confirmed' but rather 'If children have been baptized. why should not they also be eligible to participate fully in receiving the Lord's Supper'?

CBC threw down the gauntlet, which was not really picked up until *On the Way* in 1995. However, the next report, the 1988 General Synod publication entitled *Children in the Way (CITW),* was significant.

2. *Children in the Way (CITW)*

CITW did not deal specifically with the issue of children in Communion but was rather a more wide-ranging analysis of the results of a nation-wide survey of the changes in family life and education which affect children today. Of particular interest was the theological basis upon which 'initiation' and 'participation' in the community of believers was to be understood.

The report took a further step away from a covenantal approach to a less clearly defined definition of membership. Part of this shift was a very healthy concern that the church takes seriously its call to be in the society that has so changed in the post-war years. It can no longer be assumed that children will come through our doors to receive their Christian education, so mission should take place in the community, with an awareness of the need to reach whole families and provide support at whatever level children may require (see *CITW,* pp.14-25).

The report then goes on to explore three models, or ways of understanding how children are integrated into the community of faith. These are the 'school' model, the 'family' model and the 'pilgrim church' model (*CITW*, pp.26ff.).

2.1 The 'school' model

The report suggests that, whilst Christian education is still one aspect of a child's experience of church, praising God, and not just learning about him, is critical. They advocate moving away from the terminology of 'Sunday School', with a teacher imparting knowledge in an outdated pedagogical methodology: instead the *leader* should 'share a journey of faith' with the children (p.29). Whilst the 'journey' language makes me a little uncomfortable (for reasons I shall discuss in a moment), the principle is well taken.

At St Luke's we have ceased to use the term 'Sunday School' for what the young people do on a Sunday, and have instead adopted the name 'Junior Church', which is staffed by 'leaders', not teachers. We recognize that the task is not purely education but disciple-making. Consequently we look for committed believers of mature standing who will model the Christian life. We should not automatically look to those who are school teachers to lead the Junior Church group. Their teaching skills are very much needed in Junior Church of course, however we do not want merely to replicate a classroom setting but want to produce *disciples*.

2.2 The 'family' model

The picture of an ideal family, in which the members of the family support and help one another and learning takes place through the imitation of skills and attitudes, watching and listening, encouragement and acceptance, shared in a context of security, helps develop an understanding of what church is/could be like.

The weakness of this model, according to the report, relates to the danger of an inward look of self-absorption (p.32), and a concern that single people may be excluded. The report concludes: 'We need to feel free enough and confident enough to explore other models, to see what may be safely relinquished from our present approach and what may be adapted and enriched for the future' (p.33).

However, unlike the 'school' model, which has no particular support from Scripture, the 'family' model does have very strong associations with the Bible view of the church (see Gen. 7:1-13; Amos 3:2; Acts 2:39; 16:31; 1 Tim. 3:1-15). The 'household' of the church is likened to the 'household' of the family.[6]

I suggest that the main concern with the 'family' model of church is that today's isolated, fragmented and 'nuclear' perception of family life is read back into the word 'family', rather than the extended, open house, multigenerational view of 'the household' (and therefore the family) spoken of in the Bible.

I wonder whether, in the light of the third (and favoured model) which follows, part of the rejection of the 'family' model is a reflection of an unwillingness to define clearly the boundaries of membership of the church, which a 'family' model does by implication. This issue of membership becomes quite important when we consider further the basis on which we invite children to come to the Lord's Table.

2.3 The 'pilgrim' model

The 'pilgrim model' is described as a joint sharing between child and adult in which one may learn from the other. In this journey, experiences and stories can be shared and passed down the generations (p.34). Children and adults are fellow-learners. Knowledge for the journey ahead is required and communicated in the context of the joint travelling experience.

From this foundation, the report highlights ways in which Christian faith may be nourished in the community of the church. Quoting John Westerhoff, there are four style of faith which need to be recognized: 'experienced faith' (imitation and observing faith); 'affiliative faith' (participating faith); 'searching faith' (where questioning and personal doubts are dealt with); and 'owned faith' (when the faith is taken on board and held). It is this whole progress through four stages which Westerhoff sees as conversion, and the report comments: 'wherever we are on that pilgrimage, none is outside Christ's redeeming grace' (see pp.40ff.).

I have a few problems with the conclusion of this report, however.

2.3.1 First, the looseness of the journey language can imply a process without beginning and without end. When the Bible speaks of 'pilgrimage' (see 1 Peter 2:11-12), the implication is that the journey begins with Christian conversion – or if you will, the integration into the covenant community of believers through paedobaptism – and ends with the second coming of Christ or the completion of our salvation in glory. In other words, pilgrimage is a journey of the faithful, not a journey *to* faith![7]

2.3.2 Secondly, given the relatively 'open baptism' policy the Church of England is required to hold, is it sufficient to imply that full membership may be assumed as a result of baptismal initiation? The report states: 'A person refused baptism can legitimately ask how the mind and love of Christ is expressed in the refusal' (p.84). Quoting John 20:19-23, the report itself clearly seems to assume that water baptism is the agent whereby the Spirit is imparted (even though this passage probably has nothing to do with water baptism!). Moreover, even when there are strong reasons to suggest that it is the children of believing parents who are being baptized, the more biblical and covenantal understanding of membership implies that children are included in the covenant purely on the basis of the faith of their parents. In other words, their full membership needs personal and public ratification at a later date. In their minority they are junior members attending under the fully paid up membership of their parents!

2.3.3 Thirdly, I agree that experientially we may speak of stages, growth and development in our understanding of faith. Many people, myself included, cannot name a time, place or date of conversion, but experienced a change over a number of years. However, even acknowledging the journey language, we must recognize a point of pass-over from 'the journey to faith' and the 'journey of faith'!

I can point to a time when I knew I was not a Christian (for me that was an awareness of sin in my life at the age of 13), and a time when I knew I was a Christian (which happened when I believed that Jesus had died for *my sins*, I was forgiven and born anew at the age of 17. One evidence for me was a real desire to be in church and to be in the world telling others about him!). Indeed, though I may not have known the time of my conversion, to be sure, in God's eyes I passed from death to life (2 Cor. 5:17; Eph. 2:4-6; 1 John 3:14) and I was born from above (John 3:1-6) at a moment which sent the angels in heaven rejoicing!! (Luke 15:7). It was not until then that I began my pilgrimage.

3. *On The Way (OTW)*

The meaning attached to journey language is spelled out more fully in the next General Synod report *On the Way* (OTW), published in 1995, the middle of the Decade of Evangelism. The report helpfully outlines the conversion of the Apostle Paul, pointing out that the process of conversion was not complete at the moment of flashing light on the Damascus road but required the initiation into a community of believers. This happens when Paul joins the Christians in Damascus and tells the story of his own conversion.

However, again, this model reveals some inadequacies when the report concludes: 'It is while Paul is on the road that he meets the risen Christ. The idea of the journey...as an image of human life and of the passage to faith allows both for the integration of faith with human experience and for the necessity of change and development' (pp.18ff.). The use of journey language seems to imply no real certainty of which road is being travelled on, or whether one has any assurance that there is any destination in view!

However, OTW sought to bring together an integrated approach to Christian initiation which would at least in part answer the question left unanswered at the end of *CITW*. How do we get non-church adults and children on the way of faith when their exposure to church is getting less and less?

OTW engages seriously with the starting point of many who enquire about the Christian faith, whether they be parents approaching the parish vicar for baptism of their new child, or adults wishing to become Christians. The opportunities for significant spiritual input presented by baptism clearly need to be carefully addressed. In John Finney's *Finding Faith Today* it was observed that 12 per cent of men and 30 per cent of women saw their children, including the birth of a child or a request for their child's baptism, as a significant factor in their journey (cited by *OTW*, p.25). The Acts 9 passage is a good example of the 'process model' of coming to faith as much as it is a 'crisis model'. Even prior to his conversion, Saul was in intimate contact with the Christian community (Acts 7:58) and who knows what impact their witness had.

The report highlights the traditional attitude to preparation for initiation among both evangelicals and Catholics as being 'a didactic approach forged initially for the intelligent teenager' (p.15). However, it points to more recent approaches to initiation which have centred on a group life which can explore belonging and questioning. The *Alpha Course* is the most obvious and successful illustration of this 'catechumenal approach' to Christian formation. Recognizing the reality of where so many people are coming from, is critical in this process. Enquirers are coming to church with very little understanding of what the Christian faith is all about (pp.22ff.)

The report broadens into a discussion of four strands of the Christian life (evangelism, education, liturgy and ethics) demonstrating the variety of different starting points from which someone may come as a questioner or enquirer. We could spend some time discussing each of these four areas. However, the next chapter (5) is more pertinent for our discussion concerning 'children in communion'.

This section of the report is weakened by its loose usage of journeying and pilgrim language;[8] however, it is strengthened by its emphasis on an ongoing catechumenal approach to the baptism of children. Surely it is correct to identify with Ronald Dowling's three principles:

i.   The sacraments are the celebration by, of and for the gathered Christian community.

ii. Preparation for parents and godparents of infants is essential.

iii. The responsibility for the entire baptismal process, including preparation, belongs to the whole church.[9]

The report takes on board the educational and theological recognition that 'belonging is the basis of learning' (p.82). This means that we need to work hard to create a context of welcome and belonging in order to share the Christian faith. This is very typical of the post-modern approach to commitment.

Fig. 1

The 'modern' way encapsulated a process which could be summarized as 'Believe'; 'Belong'; 'Behave' (see figure 1). In other words, the entry into the community of faith happened once certain convictions had been taken on board, and then people felt as though they belonged. Christian conduct follows.

Fig. 2

However the 'postmodern' way recognizes that relationships precede such convictions, and indeed belief only happens when a sense of belonging is perceived. Hence the order is: 'Belong'; 'Believe'; 'Behave' (see figure 2).

Such an understanding of initiation is helpful so long as it is taken to refer to the doorway into a balanced Christian life which includes an integration of all the key components of belonging, believing and behaving. The fact that some people may enter through the door of belonging ahead of believing or behaving is not really an issue. However, I do not really belong if I do not believe or behave!

As I have already mentioned, I would prefer to speak of a 'journey to faith' - which implies an atmosphere of seeking, responding and being welcomed, with no expectations or obligations that come from full membership. Christian pilgrimage does not begin until after a faith commitment of some sort has been acknowledged by the individual and some public profession is made before the visible church.

This leads us on to a further question which the report itself raises. The *BCP* baptismal service, it is argued, makes no explicit demands on the faith of the parents, although it does spell out the responsibilities of the godparents (p.87). I think this analysis of the *BCP* service is fundamentally correct, with the one significant underscoring of the point that Cranmer clearly indicates: he assumes that it is *believers'* children who are being prepared for baptism.[10]

The *ASB* introduces the notion of proxy baptism, which it is argued stems from the third century onwards (although we would want to say that it has always been present in denominations holding a covenantal view of baptism). The examination of the parents' and godparents' faith commitment and example begins the baptism proper.

Subsequent to the publication of *OTW, Common Worship* initiation services have been published. In their Grove booklet on *OTW* called *Joining God's Church*, Byworth,

Read and Waller make a couple of interesting, albeit controversial, observations of the direction in which *OTW* was pointing and which was then being reflected in the draft initiation services:

> This is certainly not an abandoning of the *ASB* approach, but there is a clear shift of emphasis, softening the address to parents and sponsors *before* the baptism, but spelling out their responsibilities immediately *after* baptism, and linking this to prayer for them and their children.[11]

To this extent I believe that many Reformed-minded Anglican evangelicals find themselves more sympathetic to the now defunct *ASB* baptismal rite than either the new *Common Worship* (because it addresses the child directly not via proxies) or the older *BCP* liturgy (because though parental faith is required, the charge to the child is not couched in covenantal terms, and neither can we assume the same cultural sympathies towards committed church attendance which the *BCP* does). Clearly there are important issues for evangelicals here.

OTW turns to deal specifically with the reasons and grounds traditionally held by those who hold to covenant theology.

3.1 First, I think they misrepresent the obligations for parental faith as being purely the pedagogical basis of the nurture of the children (p.88). Covenant theology is not based solely on the vision that Christian parents are best placed to educate the children (although clearly they are!). Rather the way in which the covenant was so constructed was to view households as entire units, which God dealt with as a whole (Acts 2:39, *et. al.*).

3.2 Secondly, the report argues that because many parents' journey of faith is not starting at the point of full commitment, baptism should be used to initiate the parents to the status of an enquirer. This would commit both them and the children being baptised to a process of continuing Christian nurture. This seems to be an unfair misrepresentation of the basis of membership of the New Covenant community. We are in complete agreement that membership of the covenant is no longer tied to blood or racial descent (*OTW*, p.88f.). However, the New Testament continues to apply covenant language to the church and the household of the family (for example, 1 Tim. 3:1-13). Those inside the covenant community are dealt with by God as a whole unit. To use baptism as an initiation to the status of 'enquirer' does a serious injustice to the covenant sign of belonging for which it is intended.

I would have to say that over the dozen years in which I have been ordained, it is this attitude towards baptism which has led to my witnessing more and more Christian parents having their children dedicated (or a service of thanksgiving), awaiting their maturity to make a faith commitment of their own – the very service which I would prefer to offer to 'enquirers'. At the same time we have allowed non-believing parents to take up covenant promises which, until they are in a right relationship with Christ, do not apply to them and should be accompanied by appropriate warnings and promises!

4. Where does this leave the debate concerning the admission of children to Communion prior to confirmation?

In his booklet on the subject, entitled *Admitting Children to Communion*, Donald Allister raises a number of serious concerns about the current moves to allow children to receive Communion prior to confirmation.

4.1 First, he argues that it is often thought that the words 'we welcome you into the Lord's Family' in the *ASB* service mean more than into the 'visible family' of the church in many people's minds. He argues : 'Baptism makes you a member of the visible church but not of the invisible' (p.8).

I think that *OTW* would agree that for Anglicans holding to a theology of paedobaptism, baptism is not a complete initiation (p.93). It is an incorporation into the covenant community of the church, and therefore could by implication mean admission to a status allowing the reception of the covenant signs of grace (namely the Lord's Supper). The sign of membership of the visible church is water baptism (as circumcision was in the Old Covenant). By deduction is it not right to allow the signs of belonging to the community to be received – in principle – by all such members?

This need not imply that the transition to adult membership of the church is lost. Donald's concern about the loss of confidence in confirmation is quite right. For many it has become nothing more than an 'passing out parade'. However, if confirmation is deferred to a later date and the signs of belonging are given earlier, then we may redeem confirmation for its intended purpose – namely a ratification of a mature personal faith.

I would describe baptism as being a junior membership in the church, with an expiry date if the membership is not taken up for oneself. Donald Allister speaks of a baptized young person as 'a probationary member'. I think I would prefer to call covenant children full members with an expiry date attached to that membership. Indeed the reference Donald makes concerning the parallel between baptism and circumcision (p.9) surely leads to just the opposite conclusion. Circumcision was the admission to the Old Testament community as equally as baptism is to the New. The outward sign was never intended to convey faith under either covenant, but was a valid and complete indication of belonging (subject to ratification, again in both covenants). Surely what is happening in baptism is that we welcome covenant children into the visible church, saying: 'You are treated as full heirs of the promises of God and thought of as members of the body of Christ until such point as you choose not to ratify that for yourself'.

4.2 Secondly, Donald argues that children cannot fulfil the injunction of 1 Corinthians 11:27-29, namely that they cannot examine themselves with the seriousness with which this passage of Scripture implies. This is a powerful objection to which I would make two main responses.

4.2.1. First, a great weight of responsibility is placed on the parents. If God does indeed deal covenantly with households, then the onus of ensuring that children are prepared for Communion rests quite heavily upon the parents.

4.2.2. Secondly, it is a mistake to assume that because of their immaturity children are not able to repent fully and faithfully of their sins. Indeed the sensitive consciences of children may well make them more open to seek rectification before the elements are received.

In the preparation for reception of young people to receive Communion a number of criteria need to be borne in mind. The first issue relates to the makeup of the household and preparedness of one or more of the parents to be engaged in the nurture and preparation of the children. Secondly, some clear signs of faith and understanding that the sacrament does not work apart from the faith of the recipient is required, and that the young persons have a responsibility before God to prepare themselves for Communion. Thirdly, a system of nurture needs to implemented within the life of the church. This needs to include a process of interviewing both the parents and the candidates, and it requires some formal preparation to take place. However, it also requires some future expectation of transition in which the child comes to confirmation or some other form of public ratification. With these provisos in mind I do not feel so cautious about the whole process as Donald Allister.

5. Conclusions and implementation of new policies

When we began this discussion at St Luke's, several issues confronted us and these needed to be recognized and responded to biblically. The following statements reflect dominant views in the Church of England and not necessarily the position held by St Luke's when we first entered this debate.

5.1 A mystical view of sacraments

Clearly, if you hold to a view that Christ is really present in the bread and wine the way you approach this debate will be rather different. For such people the reception of

Holy Communion is integral to receiving Christ. We have sought to explain the Reformed understanding that the real presence of Christ is found in the heart of the believer and this faith is enlivened by the 'visible words' of the sacraments which, when rightly received, do strengthen faith.

Consequently we have sought to shift the emphasis away from a perception that children are 'missing out' if they do not receive bread and wine. Rather, and more positively, when their faith is recognized and nurtured, they may grow if they are included at the table.

5.2 A sacramental view of confirmation

There has also been a prevalent misunderstanding that the Holy Spirit is imparted through the laying on of the bishop's hands at confirmation. This is not helped by the wording of the ASB and CW 'Confirm O Lord ... by your Holy Spirit' which could led to the mistaken assumption that the bishop mystically imparts the Spirit.

Some have been more cautious about allowing children to receive Communion prior to confirmation on the grounds that they have not yet received the Holy Spirit. Indeed such a caution is right. But to assume that he comes into a person's life as a result of a bishop laying his hands on the candidate's head is as repugnant as the idea that baptismal water regenerates and consecrated bread and wine work apart from faith.

For some the issue is less crudely defined – they see no direct connection between the imparting of the Holy Spirit and the bishop laying on his hands. However, *something* happens, they argue. For these people an equally crude theology emerges. If it is tacitly assumed that baptism is rather like receiving your childhood inoculation, confirmation becomes the place where you receive your booster!

Before we allow or encourage either confirmation or the reception of Holy Communion prior to confirmation, we look for some evidence of the work of the Holy Spirit in the life of the child such as: church attendance, a willingness to examine one's heart and confess sin, and a teachable attitude. This also places a great onus on the person charged with preparing the candidate to ensure that they are being taught biblically.

5.3 A desire to include children

Much of the desire to allow children to receive Communion has arisen out of a concern to have children (of church families in particular) fully included in the life of the church. This is, of course, a very legitimate aim. One of my anxieties has been to communicate the fact that merely allowing them to come to the Communion table does not achieve it. Consequently the main reason why I have been in favour of encouraging Communion for children of believing parents is because it allows for greater involvement in the community of the church family and especially that it requires teaching and nurture from the church and the family.

5.4 A loose definition of membership

One practical problem we have recognized but not fully resolved is a common Anglican one. How do you define membership of the church? If there is to be any discipline surrounding the Lord's Table, how can that take place if there is no clear distinction between who is a member and who is not? In practice the only way we can respond to this is to work on the criterion we set out below, which distinguishes between a 'Journey to Faith' and a 'Journey of Faith'. We do not have a Communion service at the 'Early Bird Service' on the grounds that this is a service mainly for the enquirer.

6. Why have I been in favour of furthering this debate even though it has been quite controversial?

As I have researched this paper it seems to me that there are three main approaches to resolving the question: 'May children be admitted to Communion prior to confirmation?'

Option One: No, not until you may be sure that the injunctions of 1 Corinthians 11:27ff. have taken place, in practice, post-confirmation. This is the line taken by Donald Allister and many conservative evangelicals.

Option Two: Yes, all baptized children are automatically admitted to Communion. Taken to its most logical (but in my mind crudest) application, I hear of clergy taking the baby from the font to the Communion rail to receive their first Communion immediately post-baptism. Clearly this option takes no account of the objections raised by Option One, and holds to an erroneous view of the operation of the sacraments apart from believing faith, for which I find no biblical foundation.

Option Three: Yes, all covenant children who show the ability to examine themselves and are being nurtured and supported by their parents in this process may receive Communion. This does not happen automatically but requires preparation and cooperation within the church and family.

I do not think that whether or not we allow children to receive Communion is ultimately that important. Children may feel that they belong to the covenant community without receiving it. The eating of a morsel of bread and drinking a sip of wine does not incite faith, but rather it strengthens faith in those who feed spiritually on the body and blood of Christ.

However because I hold to the covenantal view of Communion which I have been outlining, I feel that it has presented me with an excellent opportunity to put together a course in Christian family nurture. The approach we have taken to Communion prior to confirmation has placed the onus of responsibility very clearly in the hands of parents with the support of the body of the church, of course. However, parents are intimately involved in teaching the faith and bringing young people up in the context of corporate public worship. This approach does take seriously the injunctions of 1 Corinthians 11.

7. Two practical changes we are implementing at St Luke's

7.1. Categories of membership

We have taken up the challenge to try to provide Christian enquirers with the experience of belonging without being a member (and prior to belief). If we wish to use the journey language, then I would want to distinguish between the 'Journey to Faith' and the 'Journey of Faith'. [12] The former allows the enquirer a non-threatening place where he or she may be integrated in the community of the church with few obligations or expectations. The obligations and expectations of covenant membership include the right to receive Communion.

We recognize three types of membership: [13]

Full members – baptized and communicant believers in regular and frequent attendance (i.e. at least every other week, preferably weekly and involved in some other midweek activity); contributing financially and in terms of ministry.

Junior members – children of the above attending Junior Church. This membership expires if they do not take up the subscription for themselves as young adults.

Associate members – those who may feel that they 'belong', even if they have not yet reached the place of full commitment. This does not yet give all the privileges or responsibilities of full membership, but does give the members a safe place to investigate the faith.

Prior to reaching the position of full membership, we want to work hard to include people and give them a chance to explore the faith. Our weekly 9.15am 'Early Bird

Service' is constructed in this way. It is jargon-free, contemporary and lively, and seeks to explain the faith simply and accessibly.

7.2 Children in Communion

As a church, St Luke's has been slowly discussing the admission of children to Communion prior to confirmation. It has taken many months to isolate some of our main concerns. These have included many of the issues raised above, and not least, the desire to include our older young people fully in the life of the church.

We have made a decision to encourage a later confirmation - late teens or even into adulthood. We have not yet decided when or how to allow those aged 7 upwards to Communion. However, we have agreed that from secondary school upwards they should be admitted to Communion prior to confirmation.

We believe that the advantage of this two-tier approach is that it gives the opportunity for the congregation, the children's family, and the young people themselves to mark a transition into a maturing faith which includes allowing them to receive Communion. At the same time it defers a full adult membership until later, once some of the stormy years of the teens have passed.

The purpose of this booklet has been to show you the path which we have trod, even though we ourselves are not yet at a final destination. It is my hope that you will find what is written helpful as you work through the implications of covenant theology for the life of your church family.

8. This journey is
not over!

When we left the station at the beginning of this booklet, our first stop was to examine some of key biblical passages which speak of the continuity between the passover and the Lord's Supper and the covenantal signs of belonging: circumcision in the Old Covenant, and baptism and the Lord's Supper in the New Covenant.

After our first stop, we asked a number of questions which arose out of the biblical theological approach to the sacraments discerned in the passages of Scripture we examined.

We concluded that baptism and the Lord's Supper are signs of membership of the covenant. The key questions raised by this supposition relate to whether 'junior members' are eligible to receive the covenant sign of Holy Communion as well as the obvious one (for paedobaptists!) of baptism.

Tentatively, we have concluded that children who belong to the covenant community may receive the covenant signs, so long as they are able to 'discern the body'.

However we are still far from a final destination. Questions concerning 'What it means to be a member of the Church of England' and 'How should due and proper preparation of the young people and families be undertaken?', remain unanswered.

Despite the slightly facetious way in which this closing section is titled, I really do hope that this is not a journey without end! I am persuaded by the arguments outlined above and hope that it will move us towards an integrated covenantal approach to Christian initiation.

Simon Vibert *is chairman of Fellowship of Word and Spirit and vicar of St Luke's Wimbledon Park in South London. He is engaged in doctoral studies at Reformed Theological Seminary, Orlando and is the author of previous FWS publications. He is married to Caroline and they have three children.*

Most of this paper has been presented in various formats for the congregation and PCC at St Luke's. Simon wishes to thank them for their patience, encouragement, editing and incisive discussions which have helped to sharpen his thinking (although all errors and miscommunication remain the fault of the author!).

NOTES

[1]   Donald Allister, *Admitting Children to Holy Communion*, Reform Booklet No. 17.

[2]   The three main Church of England Reports are: *Communion before Confirmation* (1985), *Children in the Way* (1988), and *On the Way* (1995), all published by Church House.

[3]   This discussion is dealt with during commentary on John 19. See Don Carson, *The Gospel According to John* (Leicester: IVP, 1991), pp.586ff. Also, Leon Morris, *The Gospel According to John*, (Grand Rapids: Eerdmans, 1971), additional note H (pp.774ff.) is particularly helpful.

[4]   One of the 39 Articles of Religion, the official doctrine of the Church of England to be found at the back of the *Book of Common Prayer*. Article 28 'Of the Lord's Supper' states:

The Supper of the Lord is not only a sign of the love that Christians ought to have among themselves one to another; but rather is a Sacrament of our Redemption by Christ's death: insomuch that to such as rightly, worthily, and with faith, receive the same, the Bread which we break is a partaking of the Body of Christ; and likewise the Cup of Blessing is a partaking of the Blood of Christ.

Transubstantiation (or the change of the substance of Bread and Wine) in the Supper of the Lord, cannot be proved by holy Writ; but it is repugnant to the plain words of Scripture, overthroweth the nature of a Sacrament, and hath given occasion to many superstitions.

The Body of Christ is given, taken, and eaten, in the Supper, only after an heavenly and spiritual manner. And the mean whereby the Body of Christ is received and eaten in the Supper is Faith.

The Sacrament of the Lord's Supper was not by Christ's ordinance reserved, carried about, lifted up, or worshipped.

5   Further, op.cit., Carson *The Gospel According to John,* especially commentary on John 3:5, p.194f.; and on 6:53, p.296.

6   James B. Hurley, *Man and Woman in Biblical Perspective* (Leicester: IVP,1981), pp.34ff. See also my Orthos 14 *Conduct which Honours God? The Question of Homosexuality,* published by Fellowship of Word and Spirit.

7   See below for further implications of this view of pilgrimage.

8   For example, two of the presuppositions are 'the need to recognize and respect the life experience and integrity of the individual in their journey of faith'; and 'the need of the church to see itself as a pilgrim people journeying with, supporting and welcoming the individual' (p.76).

9   Ronald L. Dowling, 'Preparing Parents for Infant Baptism', in *Growing in Newness of Life,* ed. David Holeton (Toronto: Anglican Book Centre 1993), pp.94-102.

10 The rubric of this service places a heavy emphasis on the responsibility of the covenant community of the church (with less emphasis on the parental faith than the *ASB*). However, it is also clear that this sacrament is offered to believers: *in the Baptism of Infants every Man present may be put in remembrance of his own profession made to God in his Baptism.*

11 Christopher Byworth, Charles Read, John Waller, *Joining God's Church. An Introduction to On The Way,* Grove Worship Series No. 134, (Cambridge: 1995).

12 I think that John Bunyan's famous dream *Pilgrim's Progress* does just this when the pilgrim moves from being 'Graceless' to being 'Christian' as he approaches the cross where the burden of his sin is taken from his back. There was a journey to the cross in his old name; this was followed by a journey to the celestial city as Christian.

[13] Obviously this is 'in house' language and I would not suggest that such categories
are articulated amongst enquirers.

ORTHOS

Other Papers already published by Fellowship of Word and Spirit

1 The Rule of Christ and the Kingdom of God
Paul Gardner

2* The Future Roles of Priests and Laity in Christian Ministry
James Rushton

3* Ordination for Whom?
An examination of some of the biblical texts relevant to women's ordination
Paul Gardner

4 •Power Evangelism
A pastoral and theological assessment of John Wimber's teaching
Wallace Benn & Mark Burkill

5 • Signs and Wonders in the New Testament
Rowland Moss

6 New Testament Commentaries
A bibliography for evangelical pastors and students
Paul Gardner

7* Ordination for What?
A consideration of the reality at the heart of the church
Alec Motyer

8 • Healing in the New Testament: Some General Conclusions
Rowland Moss

9 Aspects of Authority
In our message - In our preaching and counselling -
In our decision-making
James Packer

10 The Problem of Eternal Punishment
James Packer

11 Recovering the Word
The need for expository preaching today
James Philip

12 The Church in the Age of the TV Image
Dare we still preach?
Simon Vibert

13 The Baxter Model
Guidelines for pastoring today
Wallace Benn

14 Conduct which Honours God?
The questions of homosexuality
Simon Vibert

15 Evangelicals and the Word of God
Paul-André Dubois

16 Prophecy and Preaching
Acts and the church today
David Peterson

* Reprinted together under the title *The Church's Ministry*

• Reprinted together under the title *Evangelicals and the Miraculous*

Fellowship of Word and Spirit is a registered charity, no. 293159

A list of all our publications and resources may be found at
http://www.st-james.org.uk/fws/